by Belén Garrido

illustrated by Mena Dolobowsky

Harcourt

Orlando Boston Dallas Chicago San Diego

Visit *The Learning Site!*

www.harcourtschool.com

Why is family life now quite different from long ago? It is because of things that have been invented. They have made many hard jobs quite simple.

Long ago, people used fires to heat some rooms of a house. Now, people use gas or electric heaters to heat a house.

Long ago, people used candles and lanterns at night. Now, at night, people use electric lights in a house.

Long ago, people used a bucket full of water to take a quick bath. Now, people use a bathtub to take a nice, long bath.

Long ago, most boots were quite hard to put on. Now, boots zip up fast.

Long ago, people heated irons in front of a fire. Now, people use electric irons.

Long ago, people spent a lot of time cooking. They used stoves heated by fire. Now, people cook on gas and electric stoves.

Long ago, baking was hard work. Everything was mixed by hand. Now, baking is quite simple. People use electric mixers.

Long ago, food was kept fresh in an icebox. Now, most of the time, people keep food in a refrigerator.

Long ago, fine clocks chimed. People could listen to the chimes to tell the time. Now, all kinds of clocks tell the time.

Long ago, a family could have had a black and white picture. Now, we have family pictures in color.

Long ago, people could only send letters to each other. Now, people can send letters or e-mail and talk on the phone.

Long ago, young children liked to play with cars made of metal. Now, young children like to play with cars made with all kinds of things.

Long ago, people would ride on carts to get from place to place. Now, people ride bikes or drive cars to get around.

What do you think family life will be like for your grandchildren? Just picture it!